SIGNS & SYMBOLS

WRITING
AND
NUMBERS

JEAN COOKE

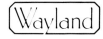

SIGNS & SYMBOLS ➤

Body Language
Codes and Ciphers
Communicating by Signs
Writing and Numbers

First published in 1990 by
Wayland (Publishers) Ltd.
61 Western Road, Hove
East Sussex BN3 1JD, England

© Copyright 1990 Wayland (Publishers) Ltd.

Series Originator: Theodore Rowland-Entwistle
Series Editor: Mike Hirst
Series Designer: Michael Morey

Cover: A girl learning to write some of the many
Chinese characters.

British Library Cataloguing in Publication Data
Cooke, Jean, *1929–*
    Writing and numbers. – (Signs and symbols).
    1. Written communication 2. Numeration
    I. Title II. Series
    302.2244

    ISBN 1 85210 903 3

Typeset by Nicola Taylor, Wayland
Printed and bound in Italy by
L.E.G.O. S.p.A., Vicenza.

CONTENTS

All the words that appear in **bold**
are explained in the glossary on page 30.

DRAWING ON THE WALLS

At school, you have probably been told never to write on the walls. But drawing on the walls was humankind's first step towards writing. Paintings in caves and on cliff faces have been found all over the world, and some were made as long as 35,000 years ago, during the **Stone Age**. They are some of the simplest ways that people have used to communicate with each other and record their experiences.

The oldest and finest cave paintings discovered so far are in south-western France and north-eastern Spain. More than a hundred of these painted caves have been found. Deep inside the caves, people drew pictures by the flickering light of simple lamps.

The caves show hunting scenes. Some of them include animals that no longer exist, such as the woolly mammoth. This animal was related to the modern elephant, but became **extinct** in Europe about 10,000 years ago. Some experts think that the pictures were made to bring good luck to the hunters. Or the paintings may have been connected with **primitive** religion.

In Australia, Aboriginal people still draw pictures on rocks, using traditional designs that are hundreds of years old.

A rock painting in France showing a hunting scene. Can you see the arrows that have been fired at the bison?

Paintings estimated to be 17,000 years old have also been found in a cave in north-eastern Brazil. Ancient rock paintings exist in North America, too. In Australia, the **Aborigines** made rock paintings at least 5,000 years ago. Today, the Aborigines regard the rocks that have these paintings on them as **sacred** sites. Some of the rocks are still used in religious ceremonies.

In Africa there are rock paintings in the Tassili Mountains of the Sahara, in Algeria. These paintings show animals that no longer live in the Sahara desert, such as antelopes and crocodiles.

A rock painting in the western USA, made by the native people of North America.

WRITING IN PICTURES

The earliest form of writing·used pictures to stand for words or ideas. It was developed about 5,500 years ago and was probably invented by the **Sumerians**, who lived in what is now southern Iraq. From Sumer the idea of picture writing spread to ancient Egypt.

Ancient Egyptian picture writing is called **hieroglyphics**, from two Greek words which mean 'sacred' and 'carving'. The Egyptians used to carve or paint hieroglyphics on their stone walls. Their civilization used this form of picture writing for about 3,000 years.

The earliest hieroglyphics were very simple. A picture stood for the thing it showed: a drawing of a stork was a stork, a wavy line represented water. But gradually the Egyptian **scribes** used their pictures to represent sounds. For example, a single wavy line stood for 'n', and three wavy lines one above the other stood for 'mw'.

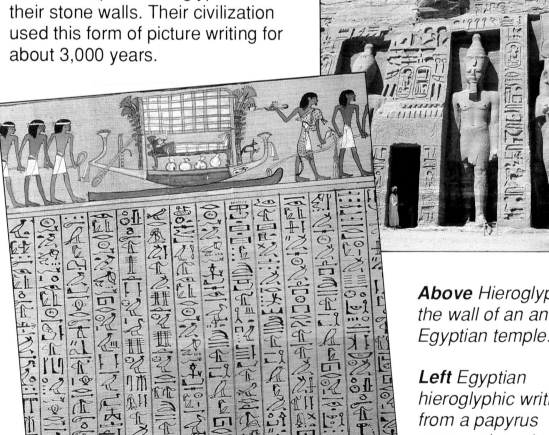

Above Hieroglyphs on the wall of an ancient Egyptian temple.

Left Egyptian hieroglyphic writing from a papyrus manuscript written about 1250 BC.

A stone wall is fine for some kinds of writing, but you cannot carry it around. So the Egyptians invented a paper-like material. It is called **papyrus** and was made from reeds that grow in the River Nile. The scribes employed by the priests wrote on papyrus with reed pens and ink. They made up a simplified version of hieroglyphics that they could write easily with a pen. It is called hieratic script, from a Greek word for 'high priest'.

Around 2,700 years ago, Egyptian scribes developed an even simpler form of writing, called demotic, which means 'of the people'. They used this form of writing for everyday business such as letters.

MAKE UP A REBUS

A rebus is a kind of coded message. Most of the words are not written down, but are replaced by pictures.

Here is a rebus:

  U at the

I saw you at the door

Here is a longer rebus. Can you work out what it means? The decoded message is on page 31.

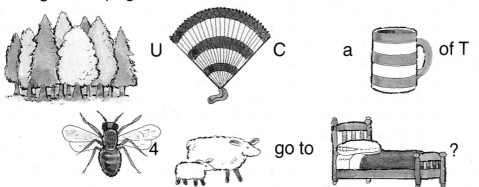

Now see if you can make up a rebus of your own, and give it to a friend to decode.

WEDGE-SHAPED WRITING

While the Egyptians developed their hieroglyphics, the Sumerians went on to a simpler form of writing. Instead of painting or carving pictures in stone, or drawing them on sheets of papyrus, they would make marks on damp clay tablets, which they then set in the sun to bake. The marks were made with a wedge-shaped tool, and this style of writing is called **cuneiform**, from a Latin word meaning 'a wedge'.

People all over south-western Asia used cuneiform writing for about 3,000 years. The Sumerians

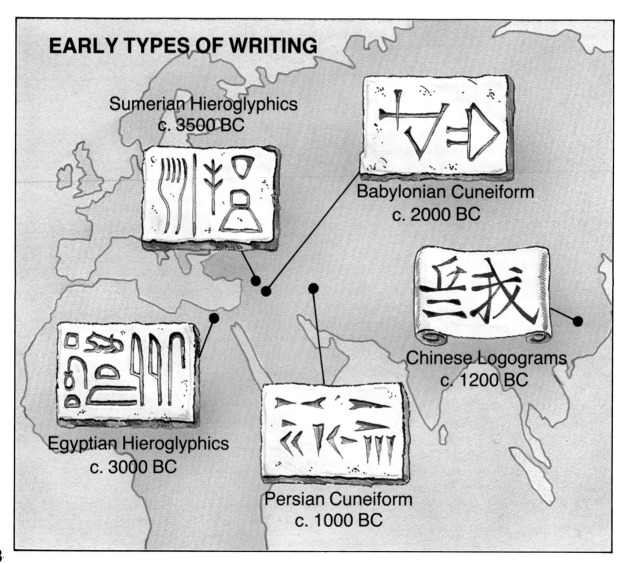

EARLY TYPES OF WRITING

Sumerian Hieroglyphics
c. 3500 BC

Babylonian Cuneiform
c. 2000 BC

Chinese Logograms
c. 1200 BC

Egyptian Hieroglyphics
c. 3000 BC

Persian Cuneiform
c. 1000 BC

A cuneiform tablet from about 850 BC. Scribes used a pointed stick, or stylus, to make wedge shapes in the damp clay.

and the **Babylonians** used about 600 different characters. After about 1000 BC, the **Persians** also adopted cuneiform writing, but cut down the number of **characters** to fewer than forty.

Clay does not rot or crumble away like paper, and thousands of cuneiform clay tablets have survived. The biggest collection was found among the ruins of the forgotten city of Ebla, in north-western Syria. It was a library of more than 15,000 tablets. The tablets include records of historical events and accounts of trade with other cities. Several tablets were the school books of a student named Azi, complete with corrections by his teacher. He learned to write so well that he became an important official in the government.

Tablets found in Iraq include the account books of merchants in Babylonia and Assyria.

CHINESE WRITING

Like the Egyptians, the ancient Chinese invented a form of picture writing. About 4,000 years ago, they developed their system of pictures to produce **logograms**, signs that stand for words. By 1200 BC, Chinese writing looked very much as it does today.

Because each sign represents a word, written Chinese has more than 50,000 characters. Some words are formed by writing two or more characters together. For example, by combining the characters for 'dog' and 'mouth', the Chinese produce the word 'bark'. They also use the same character for words that are pronounced alike, as though you used one sign to represent the two English words 'rough' and 'ruff'.

Fortunately, Chinese children do not have to learn all 50,000 characters. They need to know about 1,000 to read a very simple book, and about 10,000 to read a newspaper. A standard dictionary contains about 40,000 characters.

Although Chinese writing is complicated and difficult to learn, it does have its advantages. China is a huge country, and its one billion inhabitants speak a number of different **dialects**. Many Chinese people cannot understand each other when they speak.

Schoolchildren such as this boy in Hong Kong need to work hard to learn the many different Chinese characters.

Two boys reading a wall poster in modern Chinese script.

But because their written language stands for ideas and words, rather than how the words are pronounced, they can all read the same books. People speaking European languages have a similar system for numbers. People who cannot understand each other's speech can all read the figures 1, 2, 3, etc. These figures have the same meaning however they are pronounced, and the numbers look the same in Spanish, English or German.

Chinese characters are even used in some languages other than Chinese. Both the Koreans and Japanese borrow words from Chinese and use Chinese characters along with their own alphabets.

Unlike most other languages, Chinese can be written in columns from top to bottom.

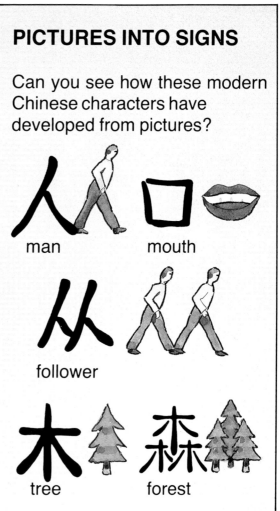

PICTURES INTO SIGNS

Can you see how these modern Chinese characters have developed from pictures?

man mouth

follower

tree forest

THE FIRST ALPHABETS

An alphabet is a series of letters, each of which stands for one or more sounds. By using an alphabet, people can write words using as few as twenty or thirty characters. Alphabets are much easier to learn than the logograms that are used in languages such as Chinese.

The earliest alphabet that we know of was invented about 3,300 years ago. Its inventors lived in **Phoenicia**, a country which was on the eastern shores of the Mediterranean Sea. The oldest letters were found on clay tablets at Ras Sharma in Syria, the site of the ancient city of Ugarit. They were written in a type of cuneiform script. This early alphabet contained thirty-two characters.

To make up their alphabet, the Phoenicians borrowed some signs from Egyptian hieroglyphic writing. They called their sign for A 'aleph', meaning ox, and used the Egyptian symbol for an ox. Their sign for B they called 'beth', meaning house, and used the Egyptian hieroglyphic sign for a house.

The ancient Greeks borrowed the idea of an alphabet from the Phoenicians. They also took the Phoenician names for the letters. 'Aleph' became 'alpha' and 'beth' became 'beta'. From these two Greek words for letters, we get the modern English word, 'alphabet'.

An inscription from Ancient Greece. Can you recognize any of the Greek letters? We still use some of them today in mathematics.

The Greeks began to use their alphabet in about 800 BC. They changed the shapes of the letters, and reduced the number of letters to twenty-four. The Greek alphabet has remained almost unchanged for about 2,300 years.

From Greece, the alphabet was taken to Italy, where it was adapted first by the **Etruscan** people and then by the Romans. With one or two alterations, this Roman alphabet is the one used by most European languages today.

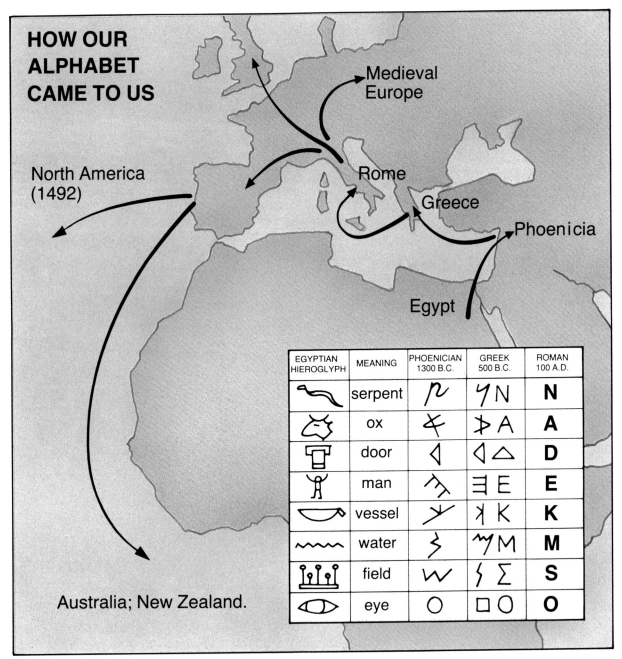

HOW OUR ALPHABET CAME TO US

Medieval Europe

North America (1492)

Rome

Greece

Phoenicia

Egypt

Australia; New Zealand.

EGYPTIAN HIEROGLYPH	MEANING	PHOENICIAN 1300 B.C.	GREEK 500 B.C.	ROMAN 100 A.D.
	serpent			N
	ox			A
	door			D
	man			E
	vessel			K
	water			M
	field			S
	eye			O

MODERN ALPHABETS

The modern English alphabet is based upon the one that was used by the Romans, although some changes have taken place over the centuries.

At first, the Roman alphabet used only capital letters. But later, as they copied books, Roman scribes invented the small letters, which are easier and quicker to write than capitals. The Romans did not use much **punctuation** either, and, as you can see from the picture to the right, often did not even leave spaces between their words.

There were only twenty-one letters in the early Roman alphabet. It did not include J, U, W, Y or Z. The Romans themselves added Y and Z later. For hundreds of years people used the letter V for both the **consonant** V and the **vowel** U, and they wrote it twice to represent a W sound. Because many scribes wrote it as UU, the letter became known as double-U. The use of separate letters for V and U did not begin until the **Renaissance** in the fifteenth century.

Although the Roman alphabet is widely used today, there are many other alphabets written in different parts of the world. Russian uses the Cyrillic alphabet, which was invented in the ninth century by the

Latin writing on the mosaic floor of a Roman villa in northern Africa. The Romans often did not leave spaces between the words like we do.

priest and missionary, St Cyril. He converted many people in eastern Europe to Christianity and also translated the Bible into the language that they spoke.

The Arabic alphabet is also used by many people, from North Africa to Pakistan. Many Indian languages are written in a form of Devanagari alphabet. This alphabet is particularly ingenious and easy to learn, because all the characters which are pronounced in a similar way are grouped together in logical order.

THE RUSSIAN ALPHABET

The Russian Alphabet has thirty-three letters:

Capital Letter	Small Letter	English Equivalent
А	а	a
Б	б	b
В	в	v
Г	г	g
Д	д	d
Е	е	ye
Ё	ё	yo
Ж	ж	zh
З	з	z
И	и	ee
Й	й	y
К	к	k
Л	л	l
М	м	m
Н	н	n
О	о	o
П	п	p
Р	р	r
С	с	s
Т	т	t
У	у	oo
Ф	ф	f
Х	х	h (as in 'loch')
Ц	ц	ts
Ч	ч	ch
Ш	ш	sh
Щ	щ	shsh
Ъ	ъ	'hard' sign, a brief pause.
Ы	ы	i
Ь	ь	'soft' y, pronounced with the letter before it.
Э	э	e
Ю	ю	yoo
Я	я	ya

Although they are written in a different alphabet, these Russian words are the same as English ones. See how many you could work out by turning to page 31.

1 Грамм
3 Турист
5 Водка
7 Телефон
9 Ресторан

2 Доллар
4 Такси
6 Парк
8 Футбол
10 Уикэнд

PRINTING

Different kinds of writing have existed for thousands of years but, until quite recently, books were very rare and expensive. Before the invention of printing, all books had to be copied out by hand, in a long and laborious process. In Europe, most books were made by monks working in monasteries. The only people who could read were the very rich and the monks themselves.

The first people to invent a form of printing were the Chinese. About 3,300 years ago, they learnt how to carve **seals** of stone or ivory. They put ink on the seals and used them to make marks on paper as signatures, just as we might use a rubber stamp today. The Chinese made the first printed book in AD 868, using a single carved wooden block for each page.

In Europe, modern printing was invented by a German goldsmith, Johannes Gutenberg, in about 1450. Gutenberg developed a system of printing which used movable type. First, he made a mould to cast the shape of individual letters in metal. He then made up a page of writing by placing the letters or characters in a frame in the correct order. The letters were inked and then pressed against a sheet of paper, to make a printed page. When one page had been printed enough times, the letters could be taken out of the frame and used again.

Gutenberg's first printing press was very simple, yet it caused great changes in people's lives. It made books much cheaper and more common, and gradually many more people learnt to read. The new books spread new ideas, and people were able to learn more about the world than had ever been possible before.

A woodcut engraving which shows an early printer's workshop. The man on the right of the picture is setting the casts of the different letters on a frame.

MAKE YOUR OWN POTATO PRINT

You will need:

    A potato
    A sharp knife
    Powder paint
    A ballpoint pen
    Paper

Safety note: Be very careful when you are using the sharp knife.

1 Cut the potato into two halves.

2 Using the ballpoint pen, draw the first letter of your name on the flat side of the potato.

3 Cut away the potato around the shape you have drawn.

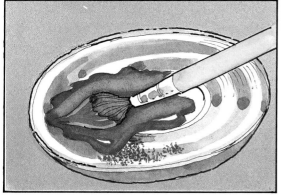

4 Mix some powder paint in an old saucer.

5 Press the potato in the paint and then onto a piece of paper, to make a print.

WRITING FOR THE BLIND

Most of us take reading and writing for granted. But some people cannot see well enough to read and write in the usual way. Instead, blind and partially sighted people have to learn special ways of reading, using their sense of touch.

The main system of writing for blind people was invented by a Frenchman, Louis Braille, who lost his sight in an accident when he was three years old. In 1824, when he was fifteen, Braille developed a code of small raised dots, punched onto stiff paper. The code is called Braille after him.

Each Braille character is made up of a group of six dots. There are sixty-three ways in which these six dots can be arranged. The Braille system includes an alphabet, numerals and all the punctuation marks. People read the characters by running their fingers over the raised dots to feel what shape they make.

As well as reading Braille, blind people can also write it, using a machine with six keys, called a Braillewriter. Or they can make the individual dots by hand, using a stylus. Braille books are produced on a special thick paper called Braillon. The characters are punched into the paper by **embossed** metal plates.

Braille is not the only type of writing for visually handicapped people. In 1845, a blind teacher, William Moon, invented a system which used simplified raised forms of ordinary Roman letters. This system is easy to learn, and so is useful for people who lose their eyesight when they are old and already know how to read. However, books in Moon type are bulkier and harder to produce than those in Braille.

Braille is not only used for writing books. This is a Braille watch. The numbers are marked with raised dots, and a blind person can tell the time by lifting the watch face and feeling the position of the hands.

18

A chart showing the Moon alphabet, a system of writing which some blind people find simpler to learn than Braille.

Royal National Institute for the Blind
Grade One Moon

A	B	C	D	E	F	G	H	I	J
1	2	3	4	5	6	7	8	9	0
K	L	M	N	O	P	Q	R	S	T
U	V	W	X	Y	Z	&	Th The	Excla-mation	?
-ing	-ment	-tion	-ness	Short stop	Full stop	Apos-trophe	Numeral	Guide lines	
Division of Verse & Italics								(Parenthesis)	

Moon Branch, Holmesdale Road, Reigate, Surrey, RH2 0BA
Telephone: Reigate (0737) 246333

THE BRAILLE ALPHABET

These are the letters of the Braille alphabet.

A B C D E F G H I J

K L M N O P Q R S T

U V X Y Z and for of the with

ch gh sh th wh ed er ou ow W

Can you work out this message written in Braille?

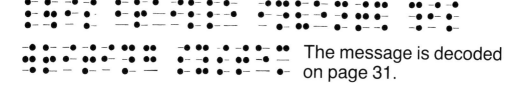

The message is decoded on page 31.

WHY WE COUNT IN TENS

Most people count in tens. They use ten symbols, called digits:

0 1 2 3 4 5 6 7 8 9

The word digit means 'finger', and that tells us why we count in tens – because we have ten fingers. Children begin counting on their fingers, and our ancestors did the same. Counting in tens has been going on for many thousands of years.

We use the ten basic digits to write all our numbers. However, the digits change their value, depending upon their place in a figure. For example, the figure 6 means six ones (6 x 1), but in the figure 60, the same digit 6 stands for six tens (6 x 10). In the figure 683, the digit 6 stands for six hundreds (6 x 100). The digit with the highest value is always that on the left.

The ten-counting system is sometimes called the decimal

Counting in tens seems to come naturally to us because we have ten fingers.

counting system, from the Latin word for ten, *decem*. We count our money in tens, which is why we call it decimal currency. All the metric weights and measures are in tens too. So there are one thousand grammes in a kilogramme. Ten millimetres make a centimetre and one hundred centimetres make one metre. There are a thousand metres in a kilometre.

Counting in tens is now the commonest way of counting, but there are several other ways of

Many countries of the world have a system of counting money in tens, called decimal currency. In the USA and Australia, there are one hundred cents in a dollar. One hundred centimes make a French franc, and one hundred sen a Japanese yen.

counting and writing numbers. As you will see in the next few pages, some different systems of counting were used by people in the past. Other ways of counting are still used in special situations today.

DIFFERENT WAYS OF COUNTING

People in some countries and cultures do not count in tens. Instead, they use different systems called bases.

The Bakairi people of central Brazil, for example, have a tradition of making up pairs in order to count. Using just two words, they have a special system of counting up to six. The Bakairi call one *tokale* and two *ahage*. Three is *ahage tokale* (2+1), four *ahage ahage* (2+2), five is *ahage ahage tokale* (2+2+1), and six is *ahage ahage ahage* (2+2+2). The San of southern Africa have three number words, and can count up to ten with them.

Computers and electronic calculators also use a special way of counting, called the binary system. This system uses just two digits, 1 and 0. It is called base two. The chart opposite explains how to convert ordinary numbers, using base ten, into binary numbers using base two.

Counting in twos is much slower than counting in tens, but computers work so fast that they perform calculations much more quickly than human brains. When they have made their calculations using the binary system, they change the numbers back into decimal digits which are easy to understand.

Computers are one of the most important uses for the binary system.

COUNTING IN TWOS

When we count in tens, we divide numbers up into different columns for hundreds, tens and units. So in the number 279, there are 2 hundreds, 7 tens and 9 units.

Hundreds	Tens	Units
2	7	9

In the binary system numbers are also divided into columns, but it uses only two digits: 0 and 1. The binary figure for one is easy: 1. But there is no symbol for two, so you have to make a special twos column, and write the number like this:

Twos	Units
1	0

You can then make the number three by having 1 in the twos column and 1 in the units:

Twos	Units
1	1

To make four, you then make another special column for fours:

Fours	Twos	Units
1	0	0

You will also need to add another column when you get to eight:

Eights	Fours	Twos	Units
1	0	0	0

Here are all the binary numbers from one to ten:

1	1	6	110
2	10	7	111
3	11	8	1000
4	100	9	1001
5	101	10	1010

Can you work out these other binary numbers over ten? (A clue is that you will need to make another column for sixteens.)

a) 12   b) 15   c) 19   d) 27

Turn to page 31 to see if you could work the numbers out.

COUNTING IN SIXTIES

Have you ever wondered why there are sixty minutes in an hour, or 360 degrees in a circle? These figures come from the ancient Babylonians and Sumerians who lived in what is now southern Iraq.

The Babylonians counted in tens up to sixty. They regarded sixty as a new base unit, and all higher numbers were counted in sixties.

The Babylonians were also among the first **astronomers**. They studied the stars and the sky, and could tell when various planets would appear to be close to or far from the Sun. They believed that the Sun moved around the Earth every year, and divided the big circle which it made into 360 (60 x 6) degrees. They then divided each

These clay tablets are almost 4,000 years old. They show problems of geometry that were solved by Babylonian mathematicians.

Do you have a protractor such as this, for measuring the number of degrees in an angle? The Babylonians were the people who decided to divide the circle into 360 degrees (written 360°).

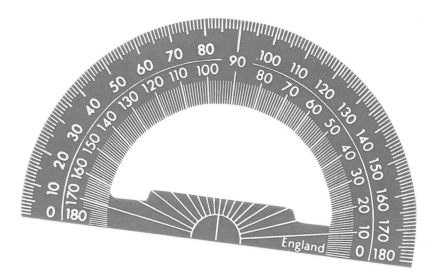

degree into sixty minutes, and each minute into sixty seconds.

The Babylonian astronomers also divided the hour into sixty minutes of time, and the time minutes into sixty seconds.

Some people, such as the ancient Aztec and Maya Indians of Mexico, had a system of counting using twenty as a second base. They probably did this because all the fingers and toes together add up to twenty. Some European people also used twenty as a special unit. The French still do: their word for eighty is *quatre-vingt* – 4 x 20.

NUMBERS IN ANCIENT BABYLON

The Babylonians wrote their numbers in cuneiform script on clay tablets. They had two symbols: ▼ stood for 1 and ◄ stood for 10. Babylonians wrote from left to right, with higher numbers first. So: ▼▼▼▼▼ was 5 and ◄ ▼▼▼ was 13. The Babylonians also used the sign ▼ for 60, but we can usually tell whether ▼ means 1 or 60 from its position.

Can you work out these cuneiform numbers?

▼ ▼ ▼ ▼ ▼ ▼ ▼

◄ ▼ ▼ ▼ ▼ ▼ ▼ ▼

◄ ◄ ◄ ◄ ◄

▼ ◄ ◄ ◄

▼ ◄ ◄ ◄ ◄

▼ ▼ ▼ ▼ ▼ ▼

You will find the answers to this Babylonian problem on page 31.

LETTERS FOR NUMBERS

The ancient Romans used letters for **numerals**. They employed just seven letters, from which they built up all the numbers. The seven letters are:

    I (1)   V (5)   X (10)   L (50)
    C (100)   D (500)   M (1,000)

The Romans wrote their numbers from left to right. The higher symbols usually come before the lower ones. So 1 = I, 2 = II, 3 = III, 6 = VI, 12 = XII and so on.

You often see Roman numerals on clock faces. Look at these numerals carefully. Can you see anything odd about the number four on this clock?

However, in any number which contains a 4 or a 9 the Romans put the lower number first, to show that you should subtract it from the higher one. For 4, the Romans wrote IV (5 minus 1). In the same way, 9 is IX (10 minus 1), 40 is XL (50 minus 10) and 400 is CD (500 minus 100).

Roman numerals have one big disadvantage. They are very difficult to do sums with! You can see the problem if you try to do this simple sum.

CXXXV + XIII

The answer is CXLVIII. But it is almost impossible for us to do the sum without converting it into ordinary numbers in our heads.

To solve their problems, the Romans and other ancient peoples relied on the abacus, a counting frame containing columns of beads strung on rods. The columns represented thousands, hundreds tens and units. The Romans did their sums by counting off the beads and moving them along the rods.

With an abacus, calculations can be made surprisingly quickly. Even today, people in China and Japan still use versions of the abacus for doing accounts and working out bills.

ROMAN NUMERALS

Roman numerals are still used a lot today. The numbers of kings and queens are shown in Roman numerals, such as Louis XVI (Louis the Sixteenth) of France or Olav V (Olav the Fifth) of Norway. In books too, you may find several pages at the beginning numbered with Roman figures. Dates are also often written in Roman numbers. For example, 1990 is MCMXC.

Here are some more dates. Can you work them out?

a) MDLXIII
b) MDCXLV
c) MDCCCXLVIII
d) MMI

Turn to page 31 to find out if you were right.

Can you work out how old this building is?

NUMBERS FROM THE EAST

The numerals which we use today, 1, 2, 3, 4, 5, 6, 7, 8 and 9, come from Asia. We call them Arabic numerals, but really they were invented by the Hindus in India, probably about the year 200 BC.

Arabic numerals are much shorter and easier to use than Roman numerals. For instance, we write 7 instead of VII, and 1,938 instead of MCMXXXVIII.

The most important thing about Arabic numerals is that their value depends on their place. For example, in the figure 111, we know at a glance that the first 1 means one hundred, the second 1 means ten and the third 1 is just one unit.

But what should we do if we wanted to write the number one hundred and one? There is no figure for the tens column. We might just leave a gap, but that could be confusing, and if we wrote carelessly, the gap would disappear. Some time about AD 500, the Hindus solved this problem. They invented the zero, 0, to mean 'nothing'. So the number

INDIAN NUMBERS

Although we have borrowed our system of numbers from India, the shapes of the numerals have changed. This is how numbers are written in India.

Can you work out these numbers?

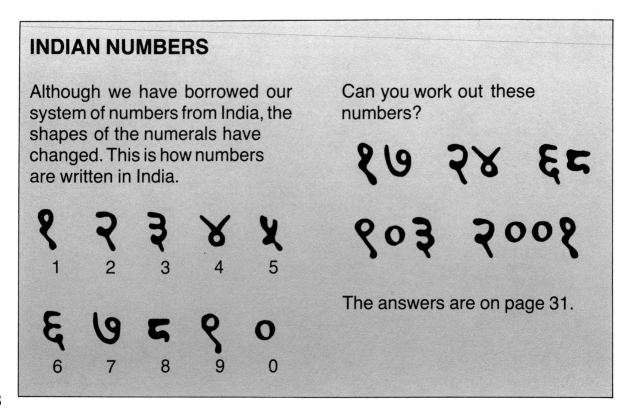

The answers are on page 31.

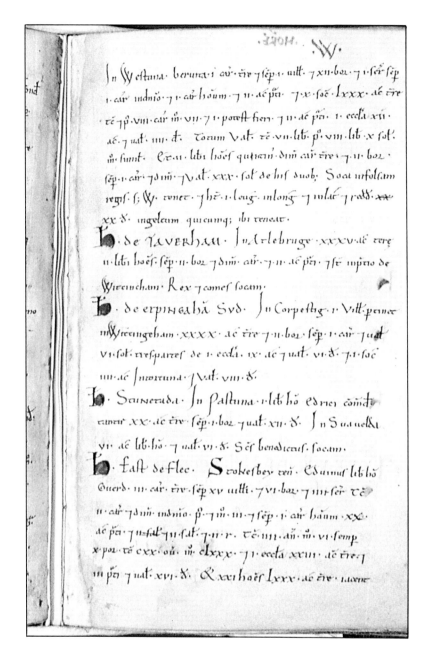

The Doomsday Book is a list of all the land and property owners in England, made by William the Conqueror after the Norman invasion in 1066. If you look at this page closely, you can see that the Normans used only Roman numerals. Because it is difficult to add up in Roman numerals, the Normans sometimes got their sums wrong!

one hundred and one can be written clearly, 101.

In AD 773, a book containing all the Hindu numerals, including zero, was brought to the court of Al-Mansur, the Arab **caliph**, or ruler, of Baghdad. The book was translated into Arabic, and Arab mathematicians began to use the Hindu numbers. Because they were so much easier to use than other systems, merchants began using them too. By the late sixteenth century, these Arabic numerals had spread to the west and were being used in Europe. Today, these numerals are used in countries all over the world.

GLOSSARY

Aborigines   The original people of Australia.

Astronomers   Scientists who study the Sun, Moon and stars.

Babylonians   People who lived in an ancient kingdom in southern Iraq, between 2200 BC and 538 BC.

Caliph   A title once used by Muslim rulers in Spain and the Middle East.

Characters   Marks, letters or symbols used in writing.

Consonant   Any letter of the alphabet other than a, e, i, o or u.

Cuneiform   Wedge-shaped writing made with a stylus on soft clay tablets.

Dialects   Local variations of a language.

Embossed   Raised above a surface by being pressed from underneath.

Etruscans   Early inhabitants of Italy, who came there from further east.

Extinct   An animal is extinct when all the members of the species have died out.

Hieroglyphics   The picture writing used by the ancient Egyptians.

Logograms   Characters that stand for syllables, words, or phrases.

Numerals   Symbols that represent numbers.

Papyrus   An early kind of paper, made from reeds.

Persians   The inhabitants of Iran in ancient times.

Phoenicia   An ancient country that flourished in the area that is now Syria, Lebanon and Israel.

Primitive   Simple, or connected with an early civilization.

Punctuation   Signs such as commas and full stops which break up sentences and make them easier to read.

Renaissance   The period of history in Europe between about 1450 and 1600, when people took a new interest in learning and science.

Sacred   Holy.

Scribe   Someone who used to write letters or make copies of books before the invention of printing.

Seal   A piece of wood or metal on which a pattern is carved. The pattern can be stamped in ink on paper, or pressed into a soft material such as wax.

Stone Age   The period when people made all their tools and weapons from stone.

Sumerians   People who, in ancient times, lived in what is now southern Iraq.

Vowel   A letter representing an open sound; in English the vowels are a, e, i, o and u.

BOOKS TO READ

Calligraphy for the Beginner by
   Tom Gourdie (A&C Black, 1983)
How Did Numbers Begin? by Harry
   and Mindel Sitomer (Harper and
   Row, 1980)

Investigating Numbers by
   E. Catherall (Wayland, 1983)
Language and Writing by Miriam
   Moss (Wayland, 1987)

DID YOU SOLVE THE PROBLEMS?

How many of the problems could you solve?

Page 7:   *Would you fancy a cup of tea before you (ewe) go to bed?*

Page 15:   1. Gramme   6. Park
            2. Dollar   7. Telephone
            3. Tourist   8. Football
            4. Taxi   9. Restaurant
            5. Vodka   10. Weekend

Page 19:   *Louis Braille invented this writing system.*

Page 23:   a) 1100   c) 10011
            b) 1111   d) 11011

Page 25:   a) 7 or 420   d) 90
            b) 17   e) 100
            c) 50   f) 6 or 360

Page 27:   a) 1563   b) 1645   c) 1848   d) 2001

Page 28:   a) 17   b) 24   c) 68   d) 903   e) 2001

PICTURE ACKNOWLEDGEMENTS

Barnaby's Picture Library 22, 26; C M Dixon Photoresources 14, 24; Eye Ubiquitous 27; Michael Holford 6 (left), 9, 12; Paul Seheult 18, 19, 20, 21, 25; Tony Stone Worldwide 6 (right); Topham Picture Library 4; Wayland Picture Library 11, 16, 29; Tim Woodcock *cover*; ZEFA 5 (both), 10. All artwork is by Stephen Wheele.

INDEX